# Religious Leadership: The 8 Rules Behind Successful Congregations

Dan Desmarques

Published by 22 Lions Bookstore, 2019.

# Copyright Page

Religious Leadership: The 8 Rules Behind Successful Congregations

By Dan Desmarques

Copyright © Dan Desmarques, 2019 (1st Ed.). All Rights Reserved.

Published by 22 Lions Bookstore and Publishing House

# About the Publisher

About the 22 Lions Bookstore:

www.22Lions.com

Facebook.com/22Lions

Twitter.com/22lionsbookshop

Instagram.com/22lionsbookshop

Pinterest.com/22lionsbookshop

# Introduction

All religions follow the same principles and you will know them in this book. These are principles that transpose time and have been in existence for thousand of years. And once you see how simple they are to apply, you will finally be able to form your own group and expand your awareness with others, while creating valuable connections that will expand your influence as a spiritual leader.

The information presented here is based on the direct experience with dozens of different religious congregations, from the most popular to the most secretive and selective.

# The Foundation of Any Religion

All religions talk about the same things. In fact, I don't think it's wise to follow one religion only. I do understand that for the vast majority it is very difficult to even understand one religion. If I tell people that they should follow at least three, they then get lost because they have no idea in which to believe. Most people need someone to tell them in what they should or not believe. And if they go to one religion and someone tells them one thing and then they go to another and hear something else, or even the opposite of what they heard before, they get lost and become confused. And so, they then can't feel integrated in a group or feel fulfilled as well. This is why most people tend to make one choice only, and when not satisfied, simply change to a new religion, and eventually might even quit all religions in general, and say: "I am an atheist and I don't believe in anything anymore."

Atheism is probably the most stupid religion in the world. Because it is indeed a religion. All atheists believe in the same things and agree on the same authors and values. And do you know why? For two reasons: One is that they end up feeling the need to fill the void in their heart with science, not a realistic one, but instead the one fed by the academia; and the second reason, is that, by not believing in spirituality, they open another void, in their mind, for the Devil to take power. And he does, through deceptive thoughts and obsessions that they then will consider natural to their nature, for lack of a better understanding. Such people then turn to promiscuity, alcohol abuse, and basically, drift way from their ideal path, losing the capacity to think effectively. They eventually start developing depression and a sense of emptiness in them, that they then need to fill with hatred for others, which turns into self-hatred. And the more self-hatred they develop, the more they project it to the outside world, as a way to detox their heart from all negativity, except that this cycle never ends, and they end up destroying themselves in this way. But because all atheists are doing the same, they find comfort in their own community of degradation, and that's indeed their congregation.

Everything we do is a choice. But just as atheism has a common ground, so do all religions. All religions are based on the same ideology.

You need to understand that most religions were created, during time periods in which humanity had very little access to knowledge or any information whatsoever. Religion was the science of ancient times. And this science was subdivided into different groups: The wisest studied religion from a higher perspective, related to numerology, cartomancy, and many other sciences that now, ironically, are seen as the occult, or evil, or even witchcraft and demonic in nature. These occult sciences that studied alchemy, and symbolism, and the meaning of the numbers, and sacred geometry, were practiced by kings and queens too. And yet, nowadays, for some reason, this knowledge is considered unacceptable and even discriminated by the masses. And even though it's just knowledge, as any other. In fact, even witchcraft in itself is just knowledge.

Why some words create a specific emotional effect, that can create a certain outcome, and why should we fear it? Why shouldn't we simply question and investigate? And what is this that we name spiritism, satanism, good and evil? How can anyone understand good without understanding evil? As a matter of fact, as I came to notice, quite too many times to be perceived as normal, demonic possession is very common in all congregations, and this happens often precisely because they refuse studying satanism and deny themselves the possibility to confront their enemy. And how can they identify that enemy, if they don't know how he looks like or manifests himself?

I've met many individuals who praise themselves as being good people, just because they follow a certain religion. And yet, they're actually selfish and very evil, and tormented by dark energies. Their evilness comes precisely from the fact that they don't know what evil is. They think that they do, but can't see that evil within them, rather than outside.

There are many religious groups in which Satan walks around freely. And many groups practice rituals, which actually attract demonic forces. There are people who go to the church every Sunday, and praise themselves as being very religious, and are possessed by demons. And I've met many of them. I've then tried to convince the members of such groups that there is someone inside, who is possessed by a demon. But do the same and see for yourself how they will react to you. They will more likely exclude you than exclude that person. This, because there's a huge amount of ignorance, in all the religions that I have encountered.

And this ignorance, is what actually allows many of the members to destroy the group. And so religion has been self-destroyed from the inside to a great extent.

What you see today are religions in the process of destruction, total annihilation, disappearing. And then you have many others that likewise have disappeared in the past. The same process has been maintaining itself for many thousands of years. All religions have several years of existence with an expiration date, just like any living organism. Congregations are indeed and simply living organisms. But then you have many other religions that are so strong, that you can predict that they'll be here for many years to come. What is also interesting about religion is that, the best groups, tend to blend with society easily, they tend to enter the social consciousness and become the mainstream among the collective of the population — they become the basis of social and cultural consciousness, or at least, a big part of it; and yet, how is that even possible, if religion did not fulfill a specific social role?

**Rule Nr.1: A religion must fulfill a social need like a single unit — a living organism, and know its enemy, as well as how the opposition, i.e., atheists, differentiate themselves.**

# How a Religion is Created

In ancient times, religions were created through compilations of books. A religion was basically an encyclopedia of knowledge. You need to understand that, in ancient times there were not many books available. There were a few papers spread around. Many times not even books. The access to ink and paper was very limited, and rare, most of which available only in the hands of the highest class. And so, it was difficult to have access even to something which was written. And, when people did have access to such writings, they would often need someone else to read for them. Because until not long ago, very few people were able to read. And that's where you get the problem and the solution provided by religion. First of all, you have very few papers available, not even many copies of manuscripts were easily available, due to the challenge of copying everything by hand; and then, people had to gather around someone with the manuscripts, a storyteller, a reader, and as few could read, few could do this job of enlightening others. And there you have the justification for the hierarchical system of religion, in which the one at the top, simplifies to a mass of ignorant souls, which can't read anything else, and need something of quick understanding, a set of rules and laws to follow. And how can you teach anything to a people who only know one book? No wonder then, that today, books that start their titles with "The 10", "The 20", "The 5", and so on, are still the most popular in market. Even God, understanding the limitation of humanity, created the 10 commandments, as if saying: "If you can't understand anything else, at least, understand this."

How can you teach people who can't even read this book but need to listen to it? Usually, in such cases, people would get around someone who could read for them. Now, many of them did not even have education because education is something very recent. And until a few centuries ago, there was not even any form of education whatsoever. The concept of education simply did not exist. The vast majority of the population, on the whole planet, was extremely ignorant. They didn't even know how to think. Most of what they knew was based on common opinions. And people are still like this nowadays, reason why so many old religions prevail. And so, we can't blame our ancestors, but say that the people in present time are very stupid. They are stupid because they have access to a vast amount of information and they neglect it on purpose.

In ancient times there was no internet, there were not many books available, and there were no public libraries. And very few libraries were even available in the entire world. And so, it was difficult to gain access to any kind of knowledge, much less science; science evolved a lot but in recent times, after removing its power also held by religion. Before there was no science but only religion and superstition. People had no idea about how life works or why something is A and not B. And so religion became the foundation of science. Religion also became the foundation of psychology. Before that, people had no idea whatsoever about how to interpret human behavior. Many priests became the first psychologists we know. It was not Freud or Jung or any other we heard about.

It was actually the priests of ancient times, even before catholicism was ever invented, that started helping people. And they could name a psychological illness as a demonic influence, but whatsoever was the name they gave to it, they would try to apply systems that many times did work. Except in specific situations in which the person was not accessible through a normal conversation. Now, this isn't very different from what psychologists of current times will do. For even psychologists today know that they can only heal people who are ready to be healed. With many other patients, all they can do is medicate them. And if they can't do even that, they'll send them to a psychiatrist that will do the exact same thing. And for this reason, what we witness now is not so different from what was happening before. We can blame them for what they did, just as much as they can blame us today for being so ignorant. This is why we need to respect religion for what it is, in its role for the development of the world, as we see it today.

**Rule Nr.2: A religion has to offer solutions to common problems, as much as it needs to educate people, promote the ability to think and encourage self-development.**

# The Purpose of Religion

Religion is behind many cultural advancements, and many procedures. Many of the first scientists were actually priests. The first astronomers were even part of Islam and Hinduism. And if we have so much information today, we can also thank the occult sciences, which brought us so much knowledge about how the world works. And I do believe that a scientist is ignorant if he neglects religion for what it is, instead of what he sees in religion. And what religion is, is the backbone of science. You can't neglect this historical background. You can question it, investigate it, but you can't neglect it. And in fact, what we're witnessing now, with Quantum Physics, is a return to this background. Because Quantum Physics is showing us, through many forms, which are known for thousand of years, even in ancient books with six thousand years old, as with the case of the Vedas from Hinduism, that we shape the world we live in by how we think. And that power of thought is exponentially increased by faith.

Indeed, the more science clarifies the truth about how life works, the more it can show us in which sections are all religions, and not only one; and how they operate, as all, being true, also neglect one part of that truth, or allow it to be simply misinterpreted.

Most of what is written in religious books, is also misunderstood, and is not necessarily false. In the end, my point is that, all religions are talking about the same thing. So how can you create a supreme religion to all others? You have two paths. And it's simple to do this. For the first part, you compile all the books, that are known today from different religions. You take a Bible, a Koran, and the Vedas, and the Bhagavad-Gita and other books, and there you have, your religion; and you can then debate all of these books. This is, for example, what Freemasons and Rosicrucians do. But you can do more than that. You see, a religion is nothing more than a compilation of texts. And you can compile your own texts. You can find the best books ever written in the whole of human history. And we never had so much access to information as today. There are millions of books available online for free. And books written more than a hundred years ago, are copyright free, which means that you can do whatever you want with them. You can also select them, and pick your favorite texts and quotes from each. Even the bible, for example, is basically just a selection of texts. You don't need to use the bible as it is.

Just as the bible complies texts, that were selected among other texts which were excluded, you can create your own bible too, by selecting texts from inside the bible, and texts from the gnostic writings compilation, which are not inside the bible, or most bibles available today; and you can compile them and create your own bible like that. And your bible can have gnostic texts that were rejected. You can create a religious book like this, and it doesn't need to match any other religious book out there. But you can do more than that as well. You can take your favorite texts from the bible, the Koran and the Hindu writings, and other groups, like Taoism, and even Buddhism, and compile them to make your own religious book.

Religion is only limited by the human mind. The truth is never limited.

**Rule Nr.3: Look at the truth as your ultimate goal, and do not exclude any information that guides you there and expands your awareness of that same truth.**

# How to Form a Group of Disciples

Now imagine that you already have your own selection of knowledge, and you wish to create your own following. To do this, you can invite friends to your house, and then talk to them about the texts you have. And once your house is full of people, instead of making a party, you could create a religion, and that's when you register your own religion, open a space of worship — a temple, and then start preaching about it. And you can then create your own rituals, rules, and eventually, you'll have your own hierarchy of preachers, that will be spreading the texts which you have selected, and sharing them. In fact, if civilization, as we see it today, is at the level it should be, and evolved enough, is because of what people would be doing in these temples. So it's actually ignorant for people of modern times, to look at ancient texts, written during a period in which most had no access to science, medical care, and much less possessed technical means of investigating their observations, and could only create philosophies about it, and consider all that the only truth necessary. That is an ignorant approach to knowledge.

We have descended a lot to a point in which we now see what were allegories and symbolism as literal facts. And no, it's not lack of faith when you claim that if archeological findings don't match scripture, then scripture is symbolic. Because if you match faith with ignorance, then you are heading towards mass schizophrenia. And you should't want that for yourself or any group, created by your or not.

If you have access to the internet, and the vast amount of writings available today, that would be an ignorant attitude. Although I can't blame those who don't. Because, here we have, millions of books, you can access to, while most people are obsessed only with one; one which we chose for either an emotional or cultural reason, because our family or country told us that such is the truth. And it is for them a truth they wish to keep, if it fulfills their best interests. For people always consider truth what pleases them.

Typically, human beings do not want the truth but only egoistical gratification. And so, they always seek the groups and the information that reinforces that, in a kind of narcissistic self-gratification, in which the God they worship is a God who actually is worshipping them back. They wouldn't be pleased to worship a God who hates them, and whom they can't possible match in any way or form. That's why idols are made in human form, and laws are broken to the lowest levels possible. And yet, that's kindergarten for someone who wishes to evolve and not waste time playing around with rituals and gatherings.

If you seek a truthful group of disciplines, honestly seeking for spiritual evolution, you must give them a truth that may be uncomfortable to them. This is what makes the difference between the religion of the masses and the cults or the secretive religions of the few. For only a few can endure the harsh truths about themselves. Only they can endure the greatest pains about their spirituality, and in doing so, also become capable or achieving the highest degrees of the soul.

**Rule Nr.4: You either create a human-like image of God that will attract the masses, or you make people worship an eternally expanding concept of truth that only attracts a minority.**

# How to Explain the Truth

When someone tells me that the bible is the only book from god, the second question I must ask this person, is: Have you ever read other religious books? If that person answers 'no' then I am certainly dealing with an ignorant soul. Because, until you read the religious books from all other religions, you can't say that the bible is the best one. In fact, if you read all the religious books out there, or a great vast amount of them, you will soon see that the bible is just one more among many sharing the same truth. All religious books talk about the same eternal glory of God. And even if you wish to deal with the topic of God and truth altogether, know that there is only one — One God and One Truth.

How you interpret God or interpret truth, is another issue to discuss. But, in a sense, we can say that it's perfectly normal to have many religions in the world. We could indeed have many more religions, sharing the same truth. And people have the right to choose the perspective in which they feel more comfortable with. But we can't say that one is superior to the others. It would be the same as to say that a white person is superior to a yellow or black person. That is ignorance. For imagine that one day, beings that are blue, grey and green, come from the sky, and show themselves superior to the whites and blacks and yellows and everyone else in between. What will we then say about them? That whoever has the green or grey color on his skin, or even blue, is superior to anyone else? And why do white people often consider themselves superior to other skin colors on Earth? All these ideas emerge from cultural perspectives. When the Roman Empire was ruling half of the known world, nobody was saying that white people were superior to black people. Because the Roman Empire was fundamentally composed of people from North Africa and the Mediterranean, i.e., what we call nowadays as brown people. And so, we can say that the Roman Empire is the Empire of the brown people.

Furthermore, if you investigate the writings of the Romans, you will see something very interesting: They considered countries seen today as predominantly Nordic, as inferior to their civilization. They said in their writings that these countries had nothing useful, were not civilized but basically composed by barbarians, which in those times meant people who don't bath, don't know how to cook proper food and eat with their hands. And they were using most of these countries, basically, as a factory for slaves — all people of blond hair and blue eyes served as slaves for the empire or concubines for the warlords and businessmen. They were taking their slaves mostly from north and east European nations. They even wrote that England for them was nothing more than forests with wild animals and ignorant people — a fertile ground only for hunting. And so, this is how much things can change in just a few centuries.

The world can change a lot and we must learn from the past. And this is how you must see religion too. Religion needs to evolve. And the best religion is the one I've just told you about — is a religion that you, yourself, created, and based on the same principles of the old religions. Because now you can indeed do that. Just don't expect people to tell you that, obviously, for it contradicts their own religious views.

What we name nowadays as seminars, workshops, conferences, in ancient times, was called a religious gathering. And of course, it can depend on the topic you are addressing. You may call it religious or not. But if you're talking about life and how it should be lived, then you're a guru, for you're teaching people how to live; and who are you to do so, unless you call yourself a guru? There's nothing wrong about it. Let others judge you as they feel.

**Rule Nr.5: Always represent the truth as the evolving unification of knowledge and people.**

# How to Be the People's Leader

Some people think that I am strange, others say I'm as an angel to them, others see me as a guru, some even believe that I am possessed by some evil spirit, or that I am crazy. I've heard all kinds of opinions about me and my work. But none of them affects me, either it is good or bad, because I am just being myself. And even though I know what I'm doing, it is sad for me, to see people who have a Masters or a PhD, putting these logos on me, which are so short minded, for they can't see someone for who he is and need to place a label on such person. And this shows me how ignorant people are even when "well-educated" or indoctrinated, depending on the perspective. My point is, right now, you have nearly eight billion people on the planet, with the vast majority being extremely stupid. And how do you deal with it? You need to rise above it. You need to move above these eight billion so that they can follow you. And you do this with any type of work; with your attitude in life, with how you talk to others and, if you wish to create a religion, also in how you see religion itself, for you will certainly be asked to comment on many others too.

You need to be above the majority and let them put their logos where they want. Allow them to place their faith where they want. Let them believe the books they choose to believe; And why not do this with books of someone alive today and help him sell more books? Why do we keep worshipping the dead rather than the living? Why do we worship the dead prophets, but not those who are alive? And why do we only value dead personalities, but not the ones living? This is something you should be thinking about. Because society and humanity, in general, need to progress, we need to move from the old to the new. And the new is nothing more than a compilation of the old, renewed and simplified — reorganized.

You will likely learn far much more from the compilations of Robin Sacredfire or Samuel Aun Weor than you will ever learn with any other religion currently on Earth. Seriously speaking, these two authors give you everything you will ever need in all fields of life, from money to love, spiritual mindsets, and much more. Beyond them, we would have to necessarily enter the field of science. And that's where Scientology is, in between both the religious and the scientific, claiming to be both and being none at the same time. Because it's actually just an unfinished bridge. If anything, what Scientology is valued for can be resumed to a few books, on the nature of the human mind. Anything else beyond that should be open for debate. And because it's not, we are dealing with a cult claiming to be religious. On the other hand, what kind of religion are all the others, who allow you to debate but not to disagree, except different cult forms? That's why I find it funny when someone tells me that Scientology is a cult. Everything is a cult. Even your friends and family become a cult when they refuse to let you think differently. Why can't people see that?

You should always follow knowledge, not agreements, for you may have to disagree in the pursuit of the truth.

Many people complain and criticize because they are lazy and don't want to be pushed forward. They wish to remain in the background, behind the curtains. They criticize the ones who know more because they feel comfortable with their own ignorance. But there are many other people who want more from life. And those are the ones in whom you should be focusing.

I don't really care about those who criticize me, because they don't affect me but themselves. When someone criticizes an author of more than four hundred books, he is exposing his ignorance, but saying truly nothing about the one he isn't entitled to judge. And yet, by doing that, they create a barrier between me and them; which means they won't read my books or learn, but move towards another path, different from mine.

Only those who can appreciate will put the efforts to know more and read more. And these ones, typically absorb everything I have to offer them, like a sponge, and apply it, and see the results for themselves, in their own life, and can judge accordingly. And well, appreciation for the things you acquire from life is what brings you more from life itself, not only physically but also spiritually speaking.

Every day, you should close your eyes and name at least ten things you are thankful for; and you should root your prayers on gratitude too, and teach your own gratitude prayers to your followers; And then, you will gain a higher vibrational stage in your body, which will, by default, attract even more good things unto you; and the same will occur to those who follow you and repeat your teachings in their own life.

**Rule Nr.6: Raise the vibration of you congregation with gratitude and never allow your followers to remain trapped in stereotypes.**

# The Political Side of Any Religion

Politics is a human invention which we created to manage human beings better. But can we truly manage people or do we need to control them? Unless politics is a system helping people move forwards and upwards in life, then what politics is doing, is controlling people. Any political systems, whatever they are doing, whatsoever we call them too, are not flawless, but always corrupted. Because the ideal political system should allow people to progress beyond it, and that won't ever happen for it means having a political system that works for its obliteration. And, by nature, the people in power, don't want to be overthrown, and stripped from that power.

This situation persists in time, as what we see currently with the situation of Catalunya. The locals want to be independent and even legally voted for it. But the government doesn't allow it, and considered any democratic act an illegal act. And for this reason, has put all politicians against it in jail. And for political reasons too, even the European Union won't recognize their independence. And yet, independence is a sign of progress. People do have the right to be independent. And when protesting in a mass scale, nobody should confront them to take that away from them.

Freedom is what comes next to independency. We should all wish to be independent; not only regarding nations but also in our personality. When people judge you because of your family background, they're stealing your independence from you. You are being your parents or family, unless you're independent from them.

When people ask others, "Where are you from?", they're stealing the sense of independence from that person, rather than recognizing it, too. For I am from where you find me, and not where I was born. Where I am is where I belong. And this applies to anyone. So when dealing with politics, we are dealing with a system based on control; And obviously, people always vote for the politicians with whom they identify the most with. That's why we can say that they get what they deserve, as there is a vibration of a certain majority that will match the vibration of the politician chosen by that same majority.

Let's not forget that Hitler came to power with the vast support of the Germans of his time. The vibration was at the same level. Not only in Germany, but also in Italy, Russia, Spain and Portugal, as you had dictators in all of these countries. The vibration of the majority was matching those leaders. And so we can blame those in power as much as we can blame the ignorant majority which allowed them such power.

The two elements — leaders and followers, are always at the same vibrational level. Therefore, to talk about politics, we need to talk first about a system of mass consciousness. For when will you ever see a politician that will want his country so highly developed that his position in power becomes outdated, unnecessary, and completely obsolete? This will never occur. Just as much as you will never have a policeman wanting peace. Because if everyone is peaceful, he won't be necessary anymore. The same thing occurs with reporters. If the whole world is in a well-balanced situation, there's nothing to report about. And the same happens with warlords, generals, soldiers and gangsters. If there is world peace, they won't be necessary.

We need to truly question the meaning of having a political system. It is deceiving to assume we can make choices, regarding being from the right, left or center. It doesn't really matter. Let's not forget that what many people now consider right extremism, is actually based on left extremism, i.e., socialism and communism. The Nazi Party was actually entitled "National Socialist German Workers' Party" and the Chinese Communism today is entitled "People's Republic of China"; but does China belong to the people? No, it doest not!

What truly matters is the human nature and the purpose of power. And that's why it doesn't make much difference if you have a monarchical power or even a dictatorship. Because, you see, a dictator who forces his people to evolve is a good dictator. And yet, you won't ever see such dictatorship in place. Because people don't want to be pushed upwards.

**Rule Nr.7: Never allow the laws of any country to dictate the moral values of your group and don't confuse power with purpose.**

# The Social Implications of a Congregation

Imagine yourself in a country where the person who rises to power forces everyone to read every single day, stops them from using television, and, imagine a dictator that doesn't want the people of his country to be stupid, but actually smarter, and he makes sure that his people eat healthy meals every day, and that nobody starves, he makes sure that education is free; moreover, imagine a dictator people protest against, but instead of killing the wisest, he kills the most ignorant. Imagine a dictator who punishes those who refuse to evolve. Imagine yourself in a country where it is mandatory for everyone to learn, read, and improve oneself. Imagine a dictator that places writers and artists in positions of power, imagine all this in a country where those same writers and artists don't need to pay taxes, and are free to earn as much as any other religious founder. Imagine a dictator saying that art is religion and giving the same rights to artists. That would be one of the greatest dictators in human history, right? Because such person would be pushing civilization, as a whole, through the influence of the energy in his country, up to a level that was never seen before. And he would be worshipped in future generations, much more evolved and capable of seeing his value and contribution to mankind, not only of his time, but many more generations to come.

You won't ever see such dictator. Because these are not the type of people in which the majority votes or the ones they appreciate. The wisest people on the planet aren't appreciated by the masses. And so, when we discuss politics, we are basically addressing personal opinions, and these are often founded on the mass consciousness of the dominating reality. What people say about politicians isn't as valid as what they say about themselves. Because they are fundamentally describing their perspective of life. And they would likely do the same they complain about if they had such power in their hands.

If you want to discuss politics, you should address a system which is progressive. And you can indeed discuss if this progress should be forced or not; but address evolution instead of politics. There's no point in debating management procedures, control methods or oppression.

We have evolved a lot since a few centuries ago, when people were being burned alive in public squares for merely reading the wrong books. We have changed a lot since then. But there is more work to be done. Because now people can read those same books and are simply not interested. In fact, when we talk about politics, we should talk from a global perspective, in how we can evolve as human beings — as a collective.

**Rule Nr.8: Dictate the ideal moral fate of a planet through the example of your leadership.**

# The 8 Rules Behind Successful Congregations

Rule Nr.1: A religion must fulfill a social need like a single unit — a living organism, and know its enemy, as well as how the opposition, i.e., atheists, differentiate themselves.

Rule Nr.2: A religion has to offer solutions to common problems, as much as it needs to educate people, promote the ability to think and encourage self-development.

Rule Nr.3: Look at the truth as your ultimate goal, and do not exclude any information that guides you there and expands your awareness of that same truth.

Rule Nr.4: You either create a human-like image of God that will attract the masses, or you make people worship an eternally expanding concept of truth that only attracts a minority.

Rule Nr.5: Always represent the truth as the evolving unification of knowledge and people.

Rule Nr.6: Raise the vibration of you congregation with gratitude and never allow your followers to remain trapped in stereotypes.

Rule Nr.7: Never allow the laws of any country to dictate the moral values of your group and don't confuse power with purpose.

Rule Nr.8: Dictate the ideal moral fate of a planet through the example of your leadership.

## About the Publisher

This book was published by the 22 Lions Bookstore.
For more books like this visit www.22Lions.com.
Join us on social media at:
Fb.com/22Lions;
Twitter.com/22lionsbookshop;
Instagram.com/22lionsbookshop;
Pinterest.com/22LionsBookshop.

www.ingramcontent.com/pod-product-compliance
Lightning Source LLC
Chambersburg PA
CBHW070739020526
44118CB00035B/1775